UNLOCK THE CHAMPION IN YOU

A LIFE SKILLS PLAYBOOK FOR STUDENT & ATHLETE SUCCESS

JEREMY "JAY" BUTLER

CONTENTS

WHY THIS BOOK

Before you get into this book, first I want to say THANK YOU, for taking the time to purchase and spend your hard hard-earned money on it. I promise to give you way more back in value than the price you spent on it.

So *"why this book"*….In total, I attended 6 different schools (2 high schools, 2 Community Colleges, and 2 Universities) and graduated from both High School and College. It wasn't until I was a 24-year-old professional athlete that I realized I had never been taught how to be SUCCESSFUL. I'll even say most people who get any form of education feel the same once they hit the real world. I know some people will say **"well... that's the parents' job"** and I was waiting on you to say that, so let's look at some statistics.

The average parent spends around 55-60 minutes per day with their children during the formative years and even less as they develop into teenagers. In total, the number is around 5 face-to-face hours per week around the world that a parent spends with their children. To show some perspective that's not even a full total day over a month. Our parents only have limited info from what their parents taught them and what their environment allowed them to pick up and learn that's where you get the generational pattern for the better or for worse. So back to "WHY I WROTE THIS BOOK," another point I want to touch on is how our idea of success is completely backwards, for example, we generally look at professionals and anybody with a college degree and or a great paying job such as Doctors, Lawyers, Athletes, and Business owners as SUCCESSFUL and that's not true at all. I know people with multi-millions of dollars, the most expensive cars and jewelry, and the biggest titles CEO, OWNER, GOAT (greatest of all time), MVP, and WORLD CHAMPION, and a lot of these people struggle with parenthood, marriage, serving others, being respectful, even more at making genuine friends and just as bad at managing the important aspects of being a person. I'm not saying achieving great things is a bad thing, the point is this, the measure of a successful person is reflected in HOW and WHO they are, not WHAT they are or WHAT they do or have. This book will define and re-shape your beliefs and habits to develop you into a SUCCESSFUL person who can develop SUCCESS in any career, especially sports. I believe this is the most important education needed for healthy prosperous lives, families, communities, businesses, and ultimately society as a whole. None of those arenas can be great without great people at the core of it. Through my own life experience and career in sports I learned 5 key principles that really helped me take control of my success in life. The 5 skills are essential to success in any area of life, basically a playbook to life success. The 5 skills I call "HIGH-5" will be the framework I share these skills to you through, so you too can have a personal playbook to become "successful" in any career you choose, but most importantly as a person. We need more champions in the world, not just the sports stars on tv, we need champions in the game of life who will shine bright and make a difference in the world. I know for a fact on the inside of every person there exists a champion waiting to be unlocked. A champion with the discipline, focus and mindset to shine bright live out the dreams and purpose that person has. This book will teach you the essential life skills to and habits to unlock that champion in you.

INTRODUCTION

Ialways wanted to write books and share wisdom, I just never knew what I would write or talk about. The more I live and Learn about Life, the more I see an issue not being addressed. We as athletes are being taught how to be great talents but not taught how to be successful PEOPLE. If you take a poll around the world and ask people…WHAT DO YOU WANT MOST OUT OF LIFE? It will always be some form of SUCCESS. As a parent myself I know what I want most for my children is to be Healthy and become successful people living successful lives, being a great athlete for sure is in the mix but it's not the most important aspect. I'm sure it's the same for all parents. Everybody has their own ideas of success and that's cool but I believe that's part of the problem. Let's imagine if we all wanted to bake a cake, let's call that cake "SUCCESS" lol, some juicy slowed-baked SUCCESS. Well if everybody has their own idea of what ingredients make this cake and what should go into this cake then the original recipe would become useless over time. We would never be able to share or pass along the recipe with anybody to get the same results. Imagine Grandma's secret fried chicken and cornbread recipe being useless after one generation. Now don't get me wrong I'm all for adding your own twists but the foundation and core of the recipe have to stay the same. So with that being said the issue I want to address is what success actually is and to share the "core" ingredients required to become just as successful of a person as we are athletes, using my own experiences and lessons from playing with and among the world's best athletes. From there you can add any special sauces or flavors to the recipe by choosing what it is you want to be successful in or at but at the CORE of success in any area of life, especially SPORTS you will find a successful PERSON. I will share and teach you what I learned on my path to becoming one of the best in the world at my craft and how you can use the same ingredients for your journey to becoming a successful person and one of the best in the world. And hopefully, you pass on the recipe to someone else.

I know a little about success myself, I achieved my childhood dream of playing in the NFL and managed to play 5 seasons coming from being an undrafted rookie. When you consider the fact that only 1% of athletes make it pro, I'd like to thank God for blessing my path and journey with that dream coming true. Playing in the NFL and being around so much personal and corporate success (on average an NFL team is worth around 4 Billion dollars) I picked up a lot of insight and behind the scene knowledge as to what **SUCCESS** really looks like, sounds like, and what real **SUCCESS** even is. The two things I learned about success hit harder than the hits I took from NFL linebackers and safeties going across the middle.

1. **SUCCESS** isn't a destination, it's a **PROCESS** of becoming.

2. It comes down to a few simple ingredients called **PRINCIPLES**, that are universal to all areas of life.

While playing in the NFL was a dream come true, especially for a young kid like myself from the lower-income side of Sarasota, Florida. The one thing I never would've guessed, was a sport I started playing in my backyard, becoming the best teacher of SUCCESS and holding the keys to my personal

SUCCESS in life and in becoming one of the best athletes in the world.

1. Leadership

2. Responsibility

3. Maturity

4. Coach-Ability

5. Team-Work

These are the principles I learned through football from the world's most successful Football players and organizations. The ingredients that can bake up a Successful person and athlete OVER AND OVER if applied.

LAYOUT

Just like any recipe, it all needs to be laid out and put in order. So here's how this book will unfold, each principle will be laid out in the chapters like this.

1. **Define**- Definition of the principle to clear up any false beliefs being held onto. We have to learn the correct play before we can run the play.

2. **Example**- Good and bad real-world examples of the principles in effect or not in effect to show the power and impact of principles. We have to see an example of the correct way to run the play on film.

3. **Apply**- How the principle can be applied to your self-development and education to maximize more of your full potential. I'll even share some areas I noticed a positive change in my life, it may be different for you, but I'd love to hear what areas you noticed a change in. GET YOUR REPS.

   DM me on INSTAGRAM or email me your testimonies and areas of improvement

IG- ButlerJay 1

Email-fillagapmentoring@gmail.com

The first half of the book will be about "YOU" and teaching you the way to career and personal SUCCESS in trying to become one of the best in this world at whatever you do. After that keep on reading I'll share my personal story and grind from a little boy with a big dream all the way to a man walking in SUCCESS.

QUICK DEFINITIONS

PURPOSE

Every person has the same purpose expressed in an unlimited number of ways and that's to fully develop and express our true potential and best selves in life.

SUCCESS

Is living in your PURPOSE; being the best version of yourself in all areas of life.

PRINCIPLES

These are universal laws built into a life that guide and protect potential into success. Think of sports with no rules or out-of-bounds markers, we need guidelines.

LEADERSHIP

DEFINED

> *The ability to bring the best out of yourself and others. i.e.,*
> *INFLUENCE*

CHAPTER 1

BE HONEST, WOULD YOU TRUST FOLLOWING A PERSON LIKE YOURSELF?

Would you trust following a person like yourself? I ask that question because most of us if not all of us in some way or another want to be known as the "LEADER". Have you ever asked yourself" Am I even a person worth following? What makes me a LEADER?

When we usually think of LEADERSHIP, I know our minds first run to whoever is put in charge or whoever has the biggest title. Up to now, that's been our idea of LEADERSHIP, but we are here to talk about real and effective LEADERSHIP. LEADERSHIP is built on inspiration and influence, you can't buy or fake inspiration or influence, it's something that people must willingly give to you. That only happens with trust and belief. Trust and belief that the Leader is capable of success. When people genuinely trust and believe in you, they become inspired and influenced to come together and give their best efforts towards a common goal with you. As a leader or in trying to become a leader you have to give people something worth trusting and believing in. To do that, first, you must show you are capable of success yourself, then you must show that you genuinely want to bring the best out of others. Otherwise, leadership can quickly turn into manipulation. Think about it, why should anybody be inspired to follow your lead if you haven't proved you're even capable of your own success?

In successful LEADERSHIP, People willingly bring the best they have to offer towards a common goal because the people are inspired by the LEADER's own success or ability. Then with that inspiration, people trust and believe this person can LEAD them into the same or more success without a doubt. Whatever can be said about what one great person can achieve alone, the greatest accomplishments in history have and will always need groups and teams of people inspired toward a common goal or vision. AKA Effective LEADERSHIP. Leadership leads to INFLUENCE.

EXAMPLE

Through some familiar sports figures, I can really paint the picture for you on LEADERSHIP. Let's look at LEADERSHIP from some of the best Leaders to ever do it in the sports world and the impact it causes.

Being a Baltimore Raven I got to experience the Ray Lewis effect. Even though he was retired by the time I came in, he would still pop into the locker room and give speeches. The dude has a gift for LEADERSHIP, he can get a room full of grown men ready for WAR. As a retired player, Ray Lewis walked into the locker room with a full three-piece suit on with no game equipment or face paint on just a suit, shades, and nice dress shoes. I literally witnessed him inspire a room full of guys to go out and kill and destroy the other team. We had guys who never jump up and down yelling or hype going into a game, excited and passionate as ever after that speech. I know because I was one of them. Ray had everybody in the locker room turned up ready to die on that field, willing to run through a brick wall. You would've thought he was about to put on some equipment and play himself. Of course, we won the game that day, we went and laid it all on the field that day for a guy who wasn't even in the battle with us. That my friends, is the power of a great LEADER. We all were Inspired and influenced by all the legendary speeches and stories we either seen or heard and of course, the work he has put in himself is what made us firm believers in him. The commitment he has to win and to be the absolute best inspires you with no hesitation to buy into his LEADERSHIP and what he demands. A lot of that has to do with how he carries himself, he demands the best and has the results to prove he will give his best effort in all he does to be the best.

Tom Brady is another Great LEADER I'm sure a lot of sports fans are familiar with. For the record, LEADERS aren't always the biggest, fastest or strongest person in the room. Tom Brady has never been the biggest, strongest, fastest, or most talented on his team since maybe little league and he'll be the first to tell you this. So that tells you it's obviously not just about those things, what Tom Brady has more than anybody else is the ability to bring the best out of whoever he works with and that skill is PRICELESS. Ask anybody who's played with or against the guy and they will tell you absolutely NOBODY can OUT-PRE-PARE him. Tom's ability to prepare allows him to play with a level of confidence that brings the best out of his skills and it even influences other guys to completely trust in his leadership and commitment to success. Think about it, would you want to let a guy like that down? He literally will call out the other team's plays and assignments for an entire game. When a person comes prepared for success, it can almost be embarrassing to be around a person like that and not be influenced to prepare yourself at a high-level to keep up. Now mix that with a Team goal or vision and boom, you get EFFECTIVE LEADERSHIP; the results speak for themselves. Tom Brady has won the SUPERBOWL more than any other player and even some entire franchises put together, with some of the most average talent that no other teams even wanted.

APPLY

So now that we understand what LEADERSHIP is and what it looks like, let's give you some real-life ways you can start applying it to see results.

Two things that stand out about Ray Lewis and Tom Brady was their EFFORT and PREPARATION. Two things you have complete control of. Ray Lewis preached 'EFFORT is between you and you, EFFORT is something you have complete control over. So why not do your absolute best in anything you do?. There ain't a force in the world outside of God that can stop you from giving your best EFFORT in anything you do. One of my favorite Bible verses is *ECCL 9:10 "whatever your hand finds to do, do it with all your might,"* you will never have any regrets in life if you do the best you can in everything you do, otherwise why even bother with it?. Doing your best has the effect of bringing the best out of you.

Tom Brady preached PREPARATION, another factor you have complete control of in all areas of life. If you prepare as best as you can, you give yourself the best chance to succeed, I don't know about you but I want the best chance of success in EVERYTHING I do, if that's not worth it to you then listen to me closely…… **THIS BOOK AIN'T FOR YOU.** It's for people who want the best for themselves and who are willing to become the best version of themselves in their life and career. Because when you put the PREPARATION in to do your best, it's contagious and influences those around you to do the same and trust your direction. Giving your best inspires others to do their best, and giving your all in preparation towards the goal inspires others to do the same and that is the result of effective LEADERSHIP.

With that being said if you start PREPARING as best as you can and giving the best EFFORT you can in all you do. The influence of LEADERSHIP will naturally begin to develop because you will begin to achieve more than you ever have and get results that you never achieved before and people will start to be inspired by you. Always remember, EFFECTIVE LEADERSHIP brings the best out of yourself 1st, then others towards a common goal. So, whether in sports or at home or in the community, or anywhere you may find yourself, you will influence and inspire the best in others and lead them toward the goals that benefit the team. Because no matter what can be achieved alone, the greatest and most valuable achievements always take TEAMWORK, and great teams always have great **LEADERSHIP.**

For reference, here are some changes I noticed once I applied the principle of LEADERSHIP to My life.

- My self-confidence increased, I was able to focus on and complete goals that I used to be scared to try.

- I was able to forgive my dad for not being present in my early years and now we have an amazing relationship

- The people around me started started to trust my leadership and advice in a way that empowered me to grow as the leader of my community.

- People within my community believed in my vision and actually started reaching out to support me and give me resources or help to bring my vision to reality. This book for example, people within my community actually helped me edit and put it all together.

RESPONSIBILITY

DEFINED

The ability to manage situations, resources, and relationships

CHAPTER 2
WHOEVER CAN BE TRUSTED WITH LITTLE, CAN BE TRUSTED WITH MUCH

There's a Biblical principal I learned from "Luke 16:10" that teaches, how you manage anything is how you manage everything. When most people think of RESPONSIBILITY, they think of who's responsible for something or who's to blame. If you're anything like me, I've always thought it was more so the person you look to when things go wrong but that's a lazy idea and the bare minimum of RESPONSIBILITY. The core of RESPONSIBILITY is 'Intentional management,' you must have clear intentions for the situations, resources, and people within your life. It takes intention to successfully manage and respond to the situations, opportunities, and resources you will be responsible for in your career, especially your life. When you don't have a clear intention for the situations you find yourself in or even things you have, you forfeit control of the outcome. You might as well just be shooting dice and gambling with your life in these areas. I don't know…. you may be built different than me, but I don't play with my life or my money like that lol. As for me, I want the best out of every situation I find myself in. I want the best resources, financial situations and relationships I can responsibly manage. In order to do that and get the best out of all situations, experiences, and resources from the game and life, you need to have an INTENTIONAL way of handling your RESPONSIBILITIES. I want to ask you this, If you don't have an INTENTIONAL plan for your money, relationships, and overall direction for your life how do you plan to achieve anything or reach any goals? Whether athletically or in life? Because if nobody has told you yet, YOUR ENTIRE LIFE AND EVERYTHING IN IT, IS YOUR RESPONSIBILITY…if you're going into the championship game, the biggest game of your life, how would you react if you asked the Head coach, what the game plan for victory was and the coach looked back at you and says….. "I don't know, I'm just going with the flow"… I know exactly what kind of look you would give coach. Same in life, the only difference is your life is the most important game you will ever play, there ain't no championship game more important than your life and it has to be that serious to you. The best of the best athletes in the world all have intentional ways of managing resources, relationships, and situations that all align with the same common goal. Which is "TO BE THE ABSOLUTE BEST THEY CAN BE". Becoming the best is not just a switch you turn on for game day, it has to be a lifestyle. Remember "whoever can be trusted with little, can be trusted with alot"

EXAMPLE

From time to time, I use sports examples and sports figures to help paint a picture, but I wrote this book to build up and help athletes learn principles from sports to become SUCCESSFUL on and off the court or field. I say that to say, in explaining principles of RESPONSIBILITY; we have to talk about and use examples of athlete stories away from the actual game. I'm not here to bash anybody, so I won't name specific people to prove a negative point or tear nobody down. I think we all are familiar with some of the mistakes athletes have made in dealing with money, relationships, and or situations where the wrong choices were made and caused way more damage than necessary, even losing their careers. With that being said let's start with money. We all know the stories and issues with athletes going broke after making millions. Outside looking in it's easy to question how it's even possible to lose so much money or to assume that the person is a reckless fool with money but let's open our minds a little…because the same thing happens just as much with the lottery winners and kids who inherit wealth from rich families. Remember the Coach question I asked earlier about going' into the championship game with no game plan to win? This is how people can run through millions of dollars, by not having an INTENTIONAL game plan for managing long-term financial success. We'll talk about solutions in the APPLY chapter coming next but let's look at another example.

I'm sure we all know and can think of at least one superstar athlete or a super-talented person who was pretty much destined for greatness but lost it all. Either by never giving themselves a chance for an opportunity or even by blowing the opportunity completely by reacting badly to a situation. The oldest example in the sports world is the people who blew it by putting themselves in risky situations that cost them EVERYTHING in some cases even their lives. A fight with the wrong people or person, hanging around the wrong crowd, disrespecting a person who has your best interest at heart such as a coach or parent, all these things affect and ruin the direction of people's lives every day, not just athletes.

It's always a sad story to see the end results but the solution to these problems is found in **RESPONSIBILITY**, having an INTENTIONAL plan for our career and lives. Think about what the best of the best athletes in the world do in becoming the best. They have an INTENTIONAL plan to be the best at what they do, and that plan overrides all resources, opportunities, and relationships that "DON'T'T BENEFIT" the IN-TENTIONAL plan of being the best. The great athletes who make the mistake of not following this plan once they achieve SUCCESS are some of the athletes we all know from the bad examples as well. So, it has to be a way of life not just a tempo-rary habit. With that being said, we now have a game plan and proven formula to follow and make adjustments for our RE-SPONSIBILITIES in handling them, and even getting them back on track when things beyond our control happen. Trust me THEY WILL HAPPEN. Just like Sports, adjustments will always have to be made to get back to the game plan. Let's roll into putting our game plan into action in the next section.

APPLY

Let's look at how we can successfully apply the principle of **RESPONSIBILITY**. In order to be SUCCESSFUL in man-aging opportunities, resources, and relationships, remember we must have an INTENTIONAL game plan. In our examples, we mentioned how some of the most successful athletes have mismanaged money and lost a fortune even going broke. Most, if not all the issues within these situations could've been avoid-ed with an INTENTIONAL game plan for their finances. The first thing needed in MANAGING money is a budget, once a budget is put in place now every dollar you make or spend is accounted for and has a role to play in your life. Learning from other people's experiences, imagine every athlete having a budget system in place. In that system, money is organized into four categories: SAVINGS, BILLS, FUN, and INVESTING. Now there's money saved and set aside for emergencies, mon-ey to cover the bills and eating, of course, we want to have a little fun here and there so that's covered with the fun account, but the investing category covers our future and helps us make money in other ways, so how can you go broke? Simple fix.

In sports, we all have "position coaches", coaches who look at our skills and talent and help us grow in the weak areas and polish up our strengths. Most importantly they hold us accountable to what we are capable of and what will make us SUCCESSFUL. In sports, we naturally yield to and allow coaches to help us and we listen to the advice given because we trust that they have the expertise we are trying to learn and apply. In life, the mindset should be the same. For example, I work with financial advisors and CPA who are my financial "position coaches" to help me organize and stick to the game plan that will lead me to financial SUCCESS, no different than my football coach, who will tell me when I'm wrong or tripping and need to re-adjust back to the fundamentals or game plan for success. If you are coachable in one area of life, allow yourself to be coach-able in all areas.

Another area to apply the tools of RESPONSIBILITY in life is within relationships with others and situations we find ourselves in. The simple way to have a plan for both areas is to first know where you are going in life, and what is the INTENTIONAL plan for SUCCESS. Once you have an IN-TENTIONAL plan for where you want your life to go, now you know what type of people can contribute to you getting there and what type of people can ruin your chances. The same goes for negative impacts on any athletic goals. If a situation or person can ruin or have a negative impact on my goals, why would I ever put myself around them or it? I haven't found one but if you have or can find a better answer, I would love to hear it. (You have my social media to connect) let me know. With an INTENTIONAL plan in place, you can clearly see how you can better manage relationships within or around your life. The same goes for opportunities, especially opportunities from others why would I do anything to jeopardize the most of an opportunity if it helps me reach my goals? I know you see my point.

As always for reference, here are some changes I noticed once I applied the principle of RESPONSIBILITY to My life.

* The experience of financial freedom is a feeling I cant really explain in words, but taking responsibility for how I managed my money allowed me to grow a sense of peace financially that I've been looking for since I was a kid growing up broke and poor.

* I now know how to make my money, make money by investing it as the budget plan says. My money literally is having money babies for me.

* All my relationships grew for the better, I found my TRIBE of like minded people because I no longer allowed anybody in my life. It got so easy to see who was really a teammate in life or who was just there for a season.

MATURITY

DEFINED

How you handle and respond to things beyond your control.

CHAPTER 3
"EVERYBODY HAS A PLAN UNTIL THEY GET HIT IN THE MOUTH"
-IRON MIKE TYSON-

Mike Tyson was asked by a reporter before a huge championship fight, "Mike, are you worried about your opponent's fight plan?" Mike's response was "Everybody has a plan until they get hit in the mouth". There is so much wisdom in that simple line. As great as Mike Tyson is and was, he lost that fight. Do you want to know why? Because Evander Holyfield responded with MATURITY by sticking to his game plan and making the proper adjustments to get back to his original game plan, even after taking the initial hit in the mouth. On your path to SUCCESS, you absolutely need an INTENTIONAL plan as to what and how you will achieve your goals. But how you respond to things beyond your control is just as important as the game plan itself. It actually might as well be considered a part of your game plan, because if sports has taught me anything, it's that game plans will never go 100% as planned. Without the ability to respond to and handle things that aren't in your game plan, you will never get back on track or to your original goals. Even with the smallest obstacles or resistance, the best game plan can crumble if the mindset and ability to respond are weak.

I grew up with the belief that MATURITY was about becoming a certain age and while that is somewhat true, it's not 100% the case. Growing up and seeing a lot of older immature adults in the world helped me understand that MATURITY is more than just age. It's about your MINDSET. When I played with the Baltimore Ravens I was introduced to this lil saying that I'll never forget, it had so much wisdom in it…"control what you can control, the game is 90% mental, and 10% physical." In simple terms, your MINDSET makes up 90% of the game. In sports, there are so many things beyond my control. I can't control the weather for the game, the fan noise, or the grass we play on, I can't control the plays being called or how the other players move or react to things. What I can control is my MINDSET in how I handle and respond to these factors. In life 90% if not more is out of your control, but how you respond and get back to the game plan after getting hit in the mouth or blindsided, is the mental side. Your intentional RESPONSE to these things determines a big part of your life's SUCCESS in any thing you do. Nobody plans for things to go wrong in life, so of course it bothers us when it does. I can 100% guarantee things in life will go wrong but how you RESPOND and get back to your INTENTIONAL plan or goal…matters so much more and that's what you need to focus on. In order to be amongst the best in the world at what you do. How you respond to adversity and obstacles on the way to your goals determines how life affects you and what happens moving forward. A lot of the same obstacles in life and sports will repeat themselves if you don't learn from them. Think about it, in the playoffs of any sport, if you can't beat an opponent or overcome the challenge, you don't get the credit and opportunity to move forward to the next challenge. Why should it be any different in life?

EXAMPLE

A little later in the book, I'll share my personal story in full so you can really see these principles at play and how they impacted my life. As an example of MATURITY I'll share this with you now, coming out of high school I had ZERO offers to play college ball…ZERO, so I went to junior college in California and absolutely hated it but it was my only chance at continuing my dream of playing division one football and making it to the NFL so I made the most of it. Coming out of junior college I finally earned some division-one football scholarships but couldn't accept them due to not having the correct classes taken. I took the classes my coaches told me I needed to graduate. Think about it, something COMPLETELY out of my control, how was I supposed to know what specific classes I needed to attend a specific university on scholarship? I had never even spoken to the university beforehand. As Tyson said, "everybody has a plan until they get hit in the mouth" and I had just got hit with a mean upper-cut to the jaw in my journey. This led to me having to sit out of school and sports for a year, then eventually going to a smaller school. I could probably throw a rock across the whole town, that's how small my school was. Being at a smaller school made my chances of living out my dream that much harder, remember only 2% of college athletes ever make it to the NFL in general. My chances had taken a big hit, probably even dropped to a negative percent chance of going pro at this point haha. Now let me show you how MATURITY in how you respond to things beyond your control can change and impact YOUR athletic journey and life. Instead of quitting or giving up because of how bad and how hard my chances of living out my childhood dream had gotten (trust me I was whining, crying and complaining for a couple of days hahaha), I focused on the one thing I had control over…MYSELF, I still had control over my EFFORT and got back on my INTENTIONAL GAME PLAN. I committed to the process and used everything that was against me as a chance to grow and improve in all the areas I fell short. I focused on getting better and better as a student, better as an athlete, and even better as a person. Do you know what ended up happening? At that same "small" school, I broke majority of my school's receiving records and became an AP All-American (the 1st in my school's history) and I guess that negative percent chance of going to the NFL was just enough. I went on to live my dream and play 5 years in the NFL, I had a better chance of getting struck by lightning 3 times in the same spot than accomplishing my goal from out of those circumstances. BUT it was my MATURITY in responding to things beyond my control. In life, some situations and experiences will seem harder than they are. In my case, they seemed impossible ha-haha, but with MATURITY you can take the hit in the mouth from life or circumstances and respond in a way that allows you to make the most out of anything even if the odds are not in your favor. In boxing, they call that a counter-punch, I took my upper-cut on the chin, and responded with a few haymakers myself to get back on track to my original goal.

APPLY

Of course, I have to give you the blueprints on how to apply the principle of MATURITY to your life. Piggybacking off the example I shared in the last section of the chapter, the key to applying MATURITY in your life is by focusing on the facts you can control regardless of how any situation comes about or how the outcome looks. Remember Ray Lewis and Tom Brady's examples, you can control your EFFORT and PREPARATION. We have 100% control over those two things. In the example above I didn't allow myself to focus on things beyond my control. I looked at the original plans of going to the NFL and took full RESPONSIBILITY for my effort and Preparation to respond to adversity in getting back on track to achieve my goals. Of course, there were factors that I couldn't change like whose fault it was, how unfair it felt, or how bad my chances were but that would be pointless. Focusing on the negative factors would've been pointless. So I used my effort and preparation to make some adjustments in getting the plan back on track. The same goes for you, you have to give complete FOCUS to the factors you have control of and give your best EFFORT to the things you can control. I promise you can turn any situation around in your favor. Factors don't determine facts they're just part of the equation, FOCUS on the factors you can control, this is the key. I'm only 31 years young, and I've seen enough in life to know a lot of things in my life felt like the worst experience and situation at the time, but turned out to be a blessing in disguise, and some of the most painful moments turned out to be the best thing that could've happened to me in achieving my goals. We don't know enough about life or the future to know how all things turn out for us. The roughest parts of our lives help shape us into the best person we could be. Allow life to happen and FOCUS and give EFFORT to how you can grow in any situation because in any situation there is an opportunity to use MATURITY and grow and learn from it. Remember, " Control what you can Control."

As always for reference, here are some changes I noticed once I applied the principle of MATURITY to My life and FOCUSED on the factors I could control.

- I stopped comparing myself to others and feeling like I was behind when I seen others on social media living "flashy" or looking successful. I was at peace with where I was in life and worked on myself day by day.

- I no longer compare myself to other people or get down when things don't go my way, I can stay cool under any pressure and perform my best

- In every situation I'm in no matter how good or bad, Im always excited and ready for the challenge because I know its just an opportunity to improve myself. Kind of like Goku in dragon ball z haha, you need to fight strong opponents in life and in sports to bring the stronger version of yourself out. I grow from every struggle in life.

COACH-ABILITY

DEFINED

> *The ability to accept instruction and correction, to be poured into for growth.*

CHAPTER 4
MICHAEL JORDAN'S SECRET TO BECOMING THE GREATEST

It goes without being said that Michael Jordan is the greatest basketball player of ALL-TIME. Air Jordan was the most dominant athlete any sport has ever seen, he literally was doing things on the basketball court that was never seen before. He was once asked by an interviewer, what was his best skill or talent that made him so great. It wasn't the jump-shot, the insane jumping talent, Michael himself said" My best skill was that I was COACHABLE, I was a sponge and aggressive to learn". Think about that for a second, the greatest most dominant basketball player ever said his COACH-ABILITY was his best skill.

We all at some point or another had a bad experience with authority or being told what to do, I know I can remember a few situations in sports or school and even at home with moms, I can almost feel those times I rebelled against moms back in the day she definitely made sure I knew better hahaha and all she wanted was what was best for me. I joke but in all seriousness, this is why we have to humble ourselves to tap into the magic that COACH-ABILITY brings. We all tend to resist being told something even if it's for our own good or if it's coming from someone with our best interests in mind.

Being COACH-ABLE allows you to learn things from people who have seen or experienced more than you, and that's an advantage I think we all could benefit from. Think about this, coaches have a perspective or view of the situation that you don't have, the "Coaches Box" literally is a bird's eye view for the coach to watch the game and see EVERYTHING so that he can give you advice and tell you things you have no view of. Once again that's an advantage I'd like to have any day of the week. Now let's look at the coach's perspective through time, most players have never been a coach meanwhile almost every coach has been a player before. That means the amount of information and experience a coach has in comparison to the player, is always greater. Imagine being able to learn and get information from experiences and situations that otherwise would be impossible for you to live in or learn from. Coaches literally can pass along 60-70 plus years of experience and lessons down to a 15-16-year-old kid. Information that took a lifetime to learn can be passed along in a 5 minutes conversation. That's the magic of COACH-ABILITY, information that may normally take you lifetimes to receive, can be passed to you through coaching within 5 minutes for you to immediately apply and make better decisions with NOW, magic right? To paint the picture for you, imagine being a 16-year-old kid having the decision-making experience and perspective on a situation equal to that of a 70-year-old adult, simply by being COACH-ABLE and allowing someone to instruct and pour into them.

EXAMPLE

Like I mentioned before I won't use any names in a negative light or bad talk anybody personally, that's not my style but to bring the point home I want to touch on a few things I think anybody with a sports background has experienced. Talent alone can almost be useless without COACH-ABILITY, I have personally seen some of the most gifted people in the world of sports sitting on the bench or being cut from the team because they have no COACH-ABILITY. The simple ability to be instructed and being able to let others help you have cost some players millions of dollars and priceless experiences and moments that they can't get a second chance at. This happens just about every week in the NFL, guys come in and have made it to the highest level of competition playing the game one specific way or playing one specific position. A coach recommends the player try it another way or even play a whole new position they've never played, of course, this can only go 1 or 2 ways in most cases. I personally know guys who were coachable and changed positions and I know guys who didn't, let's just say the guys who weren't COACHABLE, played 1-2 years at best, meanwhile, multiple guys I know who adjusted have had 10 years plus careers. Remember the magic of COACH-ABILITY, sometimes someone else may have experiences or a perspective that can help you more than you know, especially if they've been around longer, remember that. For reference don't just think football or sports, this goes with parent-to-child, respecting elderly advice, superiors at work, friend-to-friend advice, and even seeking professional coaching from advisors. Never miss out on the magic of being COACHABLE. We should all look at ourselves and see where there's room in our lives to allow others to coach us up, we all can benefit from being COACHED by someone who has the experience and our best interests in mind.

APPLY

In life, each person has 24 hours, within those 24 hours per day there's only so much information you can see and only a limited amount of time you have per day. We as people learn from our own perspectives of experiences and information. That limits how much we can learn and grow on our own. But watch this, there's only one way we can learn more without trying to make the day longer or time last longer (it's impossible, all adults have tried hahaha), and that's through the magic of COACH-ABILITY. When you allow others to instruct you and pour advice or guidance into you, you literally get to learn from other people 24 hours of life. Think about it, they share and let you borrow information and experience from all the years of their experiences and different perspectives gathered. Side note: I think that's a neat trick by God to make life this big puzzle that comes together as we connect and learn from each other, a cool and useful way to make working with others and learning from others even more special. This is how we apply COACH-ABILITY to our lives and open up the chance to grow into our full potential. We can learn anything and even learn from any mistakes we make by allowing others who've already experienced and made the mistakes before to coach us up. By seeking out people who are on similar paths or who have already had success on the path we're on, all we have to do is connect to these people and allow ourselves to be COACHED into success. Think of all the different areas within your life where you may need help, then go find someone who knows more than you and use the magic of COACH-ABILITY. It's just that simple… most of the answers and solutions to issues that hold us back in life aren't in our own minds or life experience yet. If they were then we wouldn't have the problem in the first place hahaha. The trick is that most of your solutions are sitting within the mind of someone else waiting for the magic of COACH-ABILITY to unlock it. So humble yourself and connect to others and give yourself the best chance and the biggest advantage you can have in becoming the best version of who you are.

As always for reference, here are some changes I noticed once I applied the principle of COACH-ABILITY to My life.

❖ I found myself around more successful people, people who could help me reach levels I had no idea existed. I realized the things my parents, teachers or coaches say to me was always good advice even if they yelled or said it in a way I didn't like.

❖ I started realizing everything I know, is just a very small part of all I need to know to live the life I want. I don't know everything which allows me to ask for help, help is always there we just struggle to ask for it.

❖ I was able to heal from all my childhood-pain because my dad sent me a therapist who COACHED and guided me through all the pain and hurt from my childhood and now im at peace.

❖ I realized I didn't have to go figure everything out, having people I trust to give me advice and help me, took away all the pressure of having to figure it all out alone.

TEAMWORK

DEFINED

The ability to work well and communicate with others, to achieve common goals.

CHAPTER 5
THE LEGAL STEROIDS TO SUCCESS

Another one of my favorite bible verses is Ecclesiastes 4:9-12.

"Two are better than one because they have good rewards for their work. If they fall one will lift the other." TEAMWORK is the last but maybe the most important principle because it's the foundation of all the others.

LEADERSHIP, RESPONSIBILITY, MATURITY, COACH-ABILITY all can be boosted and even made up for with teamwork. In some way or another, all of the previous principles need TEAMWORK to function at their best. Whatever can be said about the achievements or greatness one person can achieve, it's a guaranteed fact that two people can achieve more. The magic in the principle of TEAMWORK has a compound or multiplication effect. The more people you have working together, the potential result is now multiplied because the amount of work that can be done is multiplied as well. Three people can do a lot more work than two people, six people can do double the work three people can do making the reward three times bigger, see what I mean? When I think of TEAMWORK the greatest example to me that comes to mind is sports. Sports bring together people from all different walks of life, backgrounds, and cultures and get them to contribute their unique individual talent to a TEAM-specific goal. Individually sacrificing all they can giving blood, sweat, and tears to accomplish ONE common goal. It's a beautiful example of just how powerful TEAMWORK can be. To allow TEAMWORK to work its magic and be effective it requires TRUST and COMMUNICATION.

I don't know about you personally but great TEAMWORK is needed in some of the most important areas of my life: Being a great husband, Fatherhood, family, relationships, business, and even when I'm at the gym just hooping hahaha I play to win baby BALL IS LIFE. TEAMWORK is a part of our lives in so many ways already whether we recognize it or not, the question is how great or effective is the TEAMWORK surrounding the important areas of your life? Think of all the biggest goals you have in life, now think of the work it will take and the feeling of finally achieving that goal…now think of the same goal but imagine the path and feeling of achieving the goal with like-minded people who have the same goal in mind and each of you plays an important role for the group's success? Giving blood, sweat, tears even sacrifice to accomplish it together. That's the same feeling as hoisting up a championship trophy with your team. The feeling of great individual achievement is and will always be priceless, but it can be boosted and put on steroids with the power of TEAMWORK. The only thing that can make our ultimate life goals of success even better, is achieving our ultimate goals of success with a TEAM. It's the great amplifier of all accomplishments and success.

EXAMPLE

I want to throw some numbers out to help show just how much we all love TEAMWORK.

NFL Superbowl (2022) – 99.18 million viewers

NBA finals (2022) - 9.9 million viewers per game in a 7-game series.

World cup - soccer(2022) - 26 million viewers.

My point is not to convince you that these sports are better than others but in comparison to more individual sports like tennis, golf etc, or even the award ceremonies that give out individual awards such as the MVP-most valuable PLAYER award, the views aren't even close to what TEAM based sports are getting. Out of respect for individual sports, I won't even show the numbers of average game views gets in comparison. In other words, we as people love TEAMWORK and love watching "teams" compete in sports at the highest level for TEAM goals. All of us are inspired by the power and magic of TEAMWORK in some way or another. Open your mind a little so I can paint a picture of TEAMWORK, imagine way back in the caveman era when in order to eat and survive we have to hunt bison and huge animals that could even kill or hunt us. Talk about "fast food" but imagine having to literally risk your life to get some food in your stomach. This is an extreme example I know but stay with me. On any given day we can imagine a great hunter on his best days would be able to catch decent food like deer or maybe some rabbits or fish but just enough to last a day or two, on his best day. Remember all that it takes to catch food you have to hunt, kill, and carry your meal back home all while avoiding or fighting off other dangerous animals. Of course, there's a limit to what one hunter can accomplish no matter how skilled he is. Watch how TEAMWORK expands the possibility and puts the steroids into success, now imagine this same hunter goes out with a TEAM, all uniquely skilled in different ways to complement one another. Now with a TEAM and TEAMWORK, they go on a hunt and bring back a woolly mammoth hahaha, something that will feed them all for weeks or months and even provide clothing and resources. The best part is with TEAM-WORK each hunter will work less than the individual hunter has to hunt alone, each hunter's share is bigger than anything they would catch alone, and the amount of time to hunt and capture food would be shorter. I told you I would paint a great picture for you but you get the point. Whatever can be said about the skills and great accomplishments one person can achieve, it's a fact of life even way back to the caveman era all the way until now; TEAMWORK can and will always accomplish and achieve more than what one person could alone.

APPLY

Applying TEAMWORK to our lives is pretty simple. Let me show you why TEAMWORK is the foundation of all the other principles we learned. The magic of TEAMWORK allows you to bring all the principles together under one roof. Let's say you're a person who struggles with the concept of LEADERSHIP in life, no worries. If you learned anything from the last chapter you would use TEAMWORK to Partner up with someone who you felt was a great LEADER, to make up for your lack and If you are COACH-ABLE, maybe you could even learn to improve your own LEADERSHIP skills from your new teammate. Instead of always thinking you have to have everything figured out on your own or be a do it all, use TEAMWORK and ask for help. Through the power of TEAMWORK, all other principles or attributes you may be lacking can be made up for with a TEAMMATE. Allowing others to be good where you are bad and strong in areas you may be weak (for now), is not a bad thing, it takes real inner strength to admit where or when you need help. That goes for sports as well as life, if you believe in the power of TEAMWORK then you can benefit and be a part of the things you never could have done alone simply by partnering up with people who have similar goals as you. In this day and age where everybody posts EVERYTHING, please don't even think about making excuses about how hard it is to find similar people. There's this old saying I heard about TEAMWORK, which goes, "if you wanna go FAST? Go alone, but if you wanna go FAR? Go together" and it sums up the concept perfectly. Use the principle of TEAMWORK by being honest enough to ask for help when you need it or to find and partner with people who have similar goals, you will 100% always have areas where you are good and they're bad and vice versa but through TEAMWORK all the strengths of a TEAM can protect the weak areas to achieve the goal.

As always for reference, check out some of the changes I noticed once I applied the principle of TEAMWORK to My life.

- ❖ I achieved my long-term goals that I thought would take 5-10 years in 2 years with a team.

- ❖ My goals and achievements became bigger, especially since it wasn't just me working towards a goal alone. Even starting a Podcast, Writing this book, starting a business all were goals that would've taken me much longer if I stayed focused on my own efforts and abilities. I asked for help and now I have about 3-4 books ready to publish at this time, a business, mentoring program and a podcast.

- ❖ I learned to work within and with my family better, making my household run a lot smoother.

- ❖ My overall life improved by seeking therapy, financial advisors, and business coaches to teach me how to maximize the things I wanted to achieve.

CHAPTER 6
MY STORY: HISTORY LESSON FOR "5 PRINCIPLES OF SUCCESS"

"Now faith is the substance of things hoped for, the evidence of things unseen." Hebrews 11:1

Earlier in the book somewhere around the intro, I compared the HIGH-5 principles to a granny's secret recipe, so it's only right to share the "secret sauce". The secret sauce to make these principles work for you is FAITH and to be honest, FAITH is the secret sauce to make anything work in life if we're being honest. If you don't BELIEVE in anything your doing, it won't work; without FAITH you won't even believe in it long enough to allow it to work. But beyond that is faith in God, as much as it sounds cool to hear me go through so many obstacles and come out flawless and successful I'd be lying if I took the credit for it. "That's God", as you'll read in my story there are parts where logically I was at the end of the road in my journey, down so bad I mean tires flat and out of the gas at the end of the road, multiple times and things just seemed to turn around for me. "That's God", Even as athletes on the professional level amongst the best of the best in the world. There is an unspoken factor about how our talents and stories turn out that just doesn't add up or make sense how it happens or works out for us and again, "that's God". Take me for example, there are some plays in my career and some opportunities that worked out for me, where I cant begin to even explain to you how I made the catch or how things happened so perfectly on and even off the field for me to prosper. Ask any super-talented athlete or anybody with a special talent, they will tell you part of being gifted is having faith in an unknown process of how your gift even works," that's God".

So FAITH is the secret sauce that makes all of these principles work so well.

So now let me give you a little background on myself and my story and journey of development through football on to college and into the NFL and retirement after five seasons. You'll see how FAITH was the lil special sauce I used for my journey, faith in GOD was my secret add-on.

Of course, ever since I could talk and walk I was talking and walking football. I just fell in love with it before I even knew what Love felt like, whatever Love was I just knew it had to feel like my feelings for playing ball. So it felt natural to wanna go to the NFL and play against the best of the best. I get to score touchdowns on national tv and make life-changing money? Sign me up. That was a simple equation for me, I do something I love for a living plus play against the best in the world and the money is multiplied, meaning for once in my life, I get to change and control my circumstances for the better. Of course, there were some factors I never knew I was up against. Let me give you a quick fill-in of my background to bring in those factors working against me that I ignored. So the chances of going to the NFL are about slim to none, you got a better chance of getting hit by lightning twice. Of all high school athletes 6.5% go on to college on scholarship, with my background you know I needed that scholarship, we couldn't pay out of pocket. Of the 6.5% that become college athletes, only 1.2% go on to the NFL. Of that 1.2%, an even smaller amount actually stays in the NL for longer than one season, but wait, we have to factor in coming from a small country town, Sarasota, Florida. I was raised by a single mother of 4 kids(at the time, my younger sis iyanna was born later…I aint forget you sis hahah) who did what she could but the only way I was going to college was with a scholarship, even though I had my granny and uncle, and mom as my big three supporting cast, we definitely had no information or resources to make what we were going through or my path to the NFL any easier. Before me, nobody in my family had gone off to college to play ball or anything before. Now maybe or maybe not, but I say those extra factors in the equation for sure decreased my chances of living my dreams. I know for sure they ain't make it any easier. I'll pick things up around high school and go from there.

CHAPTER 7
HIGH SCHOOL: INTRO TO "LEADERSHIP 101"

The adversity I faced in high school was crazy, I was told I would never be able to play Wide-Receiver; the position I felt I was best at, we know how that story ended because it's the same position I played in the NFL. But In high school, my coaches would not let me play it, still to this day I don't know why but it led me to eventually transfer schools a couple of times to find a great opportunity. I left my original school (booker high school) left to play at a rival school, had a great game against my original school, then came back to finish my senior season. In my senior year of high school for some reason, the coaches thought it would be a great idea to not put any of my great plays and touchdowns on my film for college recruiters to see and give me a chance to earn a scholarship. I already had only a 6.5% chance of going to college I couldn't afford any more barriers to my goal. Those same coaches even further restricted us from going to college camps to be seen and scouted by coaches. It felt like these coaches were put on earth just to stop me from going to the NFL. Even though I dealt with all of that I ended up getting a chance to continue playing football at a Junior College in California, this only happened because, at the last minute, I asked my teammate who had been accepted,(TEAMWORK PRINCIPLE) if could he lend me the coaches number to send my film over, luckily he did and the rest is history. I didn't earn a scholarship, but my family didn't have to pay fully out-of-pocket tuition either, so I took it. There's a key person I want you to remember in this part of the story. I was introduced to the principle of LEADERSHIP before I even had an idea of what LEADERSHIP was. A senior football player in high school is pretty much the same way they are on tv, the cool guy on campus who got a little bit of rank on campus, just enough to feel and act above younger students, especially freshmen. We had this freshman quarterback his name was Jermaine Leverette, most other seniors were too big-time and Hollywood to even talk to a younger player, with emphasis on FRESHMAN. But he told me he respected me, thought I was cool, and that he admired my game. Instead of being arrogant and big timing him like a typical senior, I became cool and just started to share what I knew to help him become a better football player and person. I knew what it felt like to not have that mentorship and guidance in my career so I wanted to help be that for him.

Remember, LEADERSHIP is the ability to bring the best out of yourself and others. To sum it up, leadership is influence.

CHAPTER 8
JUNIOR COLLEGE: SCHOOL OF HARD KNOCKS FOR " RESPONSIBILITY "

I was technically in college but I wasn't on a scholarship so I didn't feel like I was a part of that 6.5% of kids who earn scholarships to college. Junior college made me feel every bit of how hard it was to become a part of that 6.5%. My love for the game was challenged more than I had ever been. JUCO does that to everyone, it has a way of making you prove your love and commitment to the game in ways I cant explain. I've seen and played with guys more talented than my NFL teammates, but JUCO broke their spirit to stick it out in the process. Being thousands of miles away from home, walking to school through a town of blood and crips. Similar to most JUCOs (short for junior college) there were no dorms so you had to find an apartment near campus to apply for and rent, but not as a student, no there was REAL RESPONSIBILITY and bills. I went from high school not having any serious responsibility to directly paying bills, rent, and budgeting groceries. I couldn't afford a bed so I was sleeping on an air-mattress oh and don't forget studying for classes and playing football. It didn't stop there, our meal plan with the cafeteria only let us eat two meals per day breakfast and lunch and they are closed on weekends. We were on our own as far as eating at night and on the weekend. Trying to be resourceful I went and applied locally for food stamps, it was the only way I could afford to get more food to eat. I had to lie and tell them I was near homeless, working all day but I didn't make enough to survive and that I was running out of resources to continue this way, which really wasn't a lie at all. At this point, I'm sure my chances of going to the NFL or anywhere beyond JUCO had to be around 1.5% if not negative, hahaha. This is where my FAITH was battle-tested for sure but later in life, I realized this part of my life and journey was introducing me to the principle of RESPONSIBILITY, being challenged in so many different ways showed me I had room to grow.

Towards the end of Junior college, I had gained a grip on things and ended up earning a scholarship, I received a few offers (Georgia Tech, Colorado, Tennessee martin, Lousiana-Tech, Utah state) so in my eyes, I had options, and had definitely earned myself a chance to move one step closer to my ultimate dream. I ended up committing to the University of Colorado and scheduled my first official visit. One thing I forgot to properly take RESPONSIBILITY for was my credits and classes, it was the one area I left to others who I thought knew best. Unlike what my JUCO coaches told me, you had to take specific courses for certain credits to transfer to any school, in the recruiting process I was told as long as I get my associate's degree, I could transfer out to whatever school gave me a scholarship….WRONG. So Imagine that roller coaster of feelings, literally being called to cancel a visit from the college I had committed to. To me, it was more than that, after all that hard work to get to that position and then having it snatched from under me in one phone call. I cried like a baby, but I dusted myself off and asked the only thing that came to mind…WHATS NEXT?

⚜

CHAPTER 9

SITTING OUT: DETENTION FOR STUDENT-ATHLETES TAUGHT ME MATURITY

For me, backing down from this challenge was the last option in my mind, I had already came too far. After all I just went through? No way. I had to find the next best step which was going back home and sitting out of football for a year to get my credits and classes straightened out. So I registered for classes and began training to stay in shape just in case I got in touch with an interested school that would take a shot at me. Of all the schools that offered me a scholarship before, only one stayed genuinely connected and interested and that was Tennessee Martin, the smallest most unknown school out of the bunch. Of course, I looked over them and had plans to go to a bigger school once I got my grades together. Remember the kid Jermaine Leverette, the younger quarterback from high school? Well funny how things work out. Around the time he was finishing up his senior year of high school football, I was now back home and needing a quarterback to work out and throw for me, choosing to be a LEADER back in high school as opposed to being a follower and just ignoring him look how the story came full circle. I can't help but think the way I treated him then played a part in him helping me when I needed it later. He ended up being in a position to show his LEADERSHIP. Jermaine would train with me two times per day, work out, and even play basketball for cardio, this was the best training regimen I could manage since I couldn't afford a trainer. This part of the journey taught me so much because in this chapter alone I needed RESPONSIBILITY, MATURITY, and TEAMWORK just to hang on to my dreams, the little thread it was hanging on gave me a little hope. If it were not for what I went through in JUCO, I wouldn't have been MATURE enough to respond to my situation as well as I did. I was acting and carrying myself like a student-athlete without the structure and support of a college and its resources. Although my plate was pretty full and my time all committed to the work and grind, I found a little time to get my lady pregnant. So in the midst of everything going on, I added the biggest RESPONSIBILITY challenge of all time on board. My first beautiful blessing, my son JAYSE.

CHAPTER 10

TENNESEE MARTIN: WHEN THE PLAYER IS READY, THE COACH APPEARS

Coach Simpson, Head coach of Tennessee Martin was a man of his word, he waited on me to sit out an entire year, just to get the academic side of things together. Up to this point in my life and career I had a little experience with LEADERSHIP and what being a LEADER was somewhat about. It felt like by trial and error I picked up some RESPONSIBILITY skills in JUCO after being forced to handle so many moving pieces. Of course, losing my scholarship opportunities to go play D1 college football forced a new path that required some MATURITY about how I carried myself. But even still, I had *unfilled gaps* that would be exposed in my time at "THE Tennessee Martin, WIDEOUT university" side note: I always wanted to say that on Monday Night Football Intros in front of the world. So to all my boys that played wide out at UTM: Dylan, Q, Chris aka HOOLI hahaha, Will, Rod, Malik, K.A, Roscoe, Walt, Kyle, Ben Axline, Caylon. I appreciate you, guys

I had been to college before, but going from JUCO to a University is where I learned that the difference between University and Community College life is miles apart. A university college felt like being on another planet compared to my experience at JUCO. The café opened all week except for Sundays, we even had Chic-Fil-A in the café. Compared to JUCO there were way more students, we had dorms and off-campus housing and I didn't have to walk through neighborhoods to get to class. All of that was so new and eye-opening to me, but I had never had structure and accountability like this before either. Great power comes with even greater responsibility. Adjusting to a higher level of responsibility and accountability was a bumpy road for me, I had some run-ins and some arguments with my coaches during my first year. JUCO was so poorly run, it felt like extended high school but at university, coaches were so detailed and precise with what they expected that everything I did or was doing felt wrong or like a mistake. I had never been critiqued and held to a standard that high before, let alone by a man expecting and demanding my best EVERDAY. That was new to me so, I responded how most young black men raised by a single mom would react to authority, I rebelled. I mean it was the first time I had really been pushed to do better than Good, let alone by a man I'm not even related to, why should I trust him? The majority of all athletes know the saying "If a coach is hard on you it's because he believes in you, it's when he isn't hard on you that you should worry." It's 100% true, coaching and holding someone accountable to be the best they can become is respect and love. It just doesn't feel that way when you are going through it, AT ALL. A quick flashback, In JUCO I had a great wide out coach, COACH JACK. He was a special guy man, he was the first coach to believe in me and VALIDATE my talent. (that's a big thing for us young men raised by just our mothers it's like a rite of passage into manhood.

To this day I still always check in and give thanks and pay respect to COACH JACK for how he helped me. I say that to say I had never been really pushed to be the best I could before, I didn't know how to respond to COACHING at all, and

I'm sure most young men without father figures or role models respond or will respond by rebelling as I did. A couple of one-on-one conversations with Coach Felus, who was my position coach at the time, showed me his experience in coaching and helping guys make it to the NFL. He showed me his experience studying and learning the game, he had more knowledge about the game of football than I ever thought was possible to learn. He had been studying the game way longer than I had even played football myself. He even showed me his plan to help players like myself improve. He showed me he believed that I could achieve my NFL goals and that he wanted to help me, so I lowered my guard and accepted the COACHING. Once we had that UNDERSTANDING in place, I never reacted to COACHING negatively again. If someone believes in you enough to hold you accountable to your best and help you achieve your goals, why would that ever bother you? If becoming your best is the goal. Remember Michael Jordan's best skill?

CHAPTER 11
TEAMWORK MAKES THE DREAM WORK

After doing my thing in college I finally scratched, clawed, and earned my way into that 2% of athletes in college, that go on to play in the NFL. I had finally arrived at my moment, THE BIG STAGE. Before I share what finally achieving my dreams felt like, remember earlier in the book I mentioned that TEAMWORK was the foundation of all the other PRINCIPLES, let me show you how TEAMWORK connected the dots to so many important parts of my journey and ability to master the principles of SUCCESS. Let my story be an example of how the power of TEAMWORK unlocks the most powerful resource we as humans have in each other. Sports taught me so many different things but it really taught me how to become a man, first by exposing the weak areas in my childhood and development up till that point. I had to go through everything I went through to become the man I am today. I wasn't always a great LEADER, I actually used to be shy to speak up since I was made fun of for my voice. Imagine going from a squeaky 13-year-old voice to a deep Barry White voice overnight, I was terrified just to say hello to people. I for sure wasn't always as MATURE. I came from a broken home, I watched my mom struggle to raise me and my siblings with little to no money, I witnessed my mom constantly fight with her boyfriend physically, I had old used clothes to wear to school, and my mom's boyfriend literally took our Christmas tree and gifts out of our home the day of Christmas, he bought it so he felt he could. So I was never confident or secure about my place in this world. I never developed trust in others to help me because I had so many examples and reasons not to from my journey. In my eyes there was nothing in my life worth celebrating so of course I felt insecure. I used to be terrified of RESPONSIBILITY for anything let alone money, I never had anything worth being responsible with or for. Being raised without a father and witnessing my mom's boyfriend showed me firsthand how abusive a man with power can be, I never let my guard down to anybody to embrace COACH-ABLITY, I figured nobody outside of the family would ever care enough. I say all that to expose the huge gaps within my own development and life and in sports, the only thing that gave me a chance at *FILL'N THE GAPS* was TEAMWORK, by way of sports. Sports saved my life.

It was TEAMWORK that connected and gave me an opportunity to be a LEADER to the young kid at the time of Jermaine Leverette, I had no idea at the time but as you remember Jermaine ended up playing an important role in my journey when I had to sit out of football and wait for another opportunity. Without his role in my life, I may not go to the NFL at all. Being a LEADER is simply being a great person. I owe that to my big three Granny Alice, My Mom, and Uncle Bill for always making sure to be a good person to others, "Always treat people good on your way up because you never know who you will need on your way down". My granny would always say "be kind to people, you never know when you may be talking to an angel"

During my time in Junior College, I was forced into real adult-like RESPONSIBILITIES, but without the help of my roommates/teammates Eric and Enadje, I would have never survived. My mom would've pulled the plug on my college journey had she known what my real circumstances were. I was the youngest so those guys looked out for me and through the power of TEAMWORK helped me learn to manage bills and resources and we even worked together to make our food and money last longer. They even taught me how to cook since it was my first time having to fend for myself without momma's cooking. At the end of the day I would've failed had I been alone no doubt about it.

During the year I had to sit out, my MATURITY was really tested, and everything I had been working for and towards had been put at a standstill. I could've taken that year off and relaxed or focused on all the negative things, like the people who laughed and thought I was a failure for not finishing school and not making it to the NFL, a lot of people wrote me off but their pen don't write my story. Instead, I focused on the people and things that were in my favor like my boy none other than Jermaine being in a position to help me train and work on my game while sitting out. "Always treat people well on your way up because you never know who you will need on your way down." My family's favorite quote never held so much weight as it did now. This was a time when a lot of people looked at this as my falling from grace period, falling right back down into the pit of failure I came from. TEAMWORK came to save the day again, there were people ready to help and contribute to me staying in shape and getting eligible for my next opportunity. Guess who was leading the charge? My boy Jermaine, this was his leadership opportunity within his own life, it took MATURITY to ask for help but through TEAM-WORK my mom made sure I had money and transportation, Jermaine got us access to our old high school field and weight room for workouts, a local trainer at the time Charles Chestnut would train and stretch us for free by the way he's a big time trainer now, I love his story (I'll convince him to write a book). A couple of my friends would even come out and record my training so we could see where I made mistakes or had to improve. I even had help with studying for my classes. I literally had everything I needed to overcome a situation that ends 95% of people's careers. It took MATURITY for me to admit I needed help in my situation and TEAMWORK to work with the people who stepped up for me, TEAMWORK allowed me to reap the benefits of others' strengths in the areas I was weak during one of the most vulnerable times of my journey.

TEAMWORK allowed me to let go of my stubbornness and finally be coachable, once I learned that Coach Felus wanted to help me achieve the things I already wanted to achieve myself, he showed me he truly believed in me and that he was on my team. It gave me a chance to feel validation, something I had never felt all my life, validation that I was worthy of the things I believed in. After that, the idea of being coached became TEAMWORK to reach common goals. This allowed me to develop COACH-ABILITY and gave me a chance to really grow and be poured into. I don't know how I ever thought I was going to be successful in the NFL or even life, without being coachable or willing to accept coaching but thank God for TEAMWORK.

So let's recap before we stroll into the NFL chapter of my journey, being a LEADER in high school connected me to Jermaine, not receiving a scholarship and having to go to Junior College gave me a lesson in RESPONSIBILITY, where I learned so much from my roommates. Most of my MATURITY as a young man was tested and earned when I had to sit out a year of playing ball, Jermaine came back in to save the day. Finally earning a D1 scholarship tested me before it blessed me, I struggled but eventually developed some COACH-ABILITY through Coach Felus. Last but for sure not least is TEAMWORK every person I connected with was due to some form of TEAMWORK at that part of the journey. To this day I am just as much connected to all of these people, we continue being teammates in life by supporting and helping each other in anything we're involved in.

CHAPTER 12

DREAMS DO COME TRUE: FINAL EXAMS BEFORE GRADUATION INTO SUCCESS

Flash forward hahaha I don't know if that's a thing in books but it sounds cool for a movie scene, let me tell you a few things your boy ended up doing in college that got me the NFL opportunity. In just two seasons at a university, I had 140 catches, 1953 receiving yards, and 20 touchdowns all in about 20 games, and went on to be named male athlete of the year as well. A big stamp of validation for my talent was being named All-American by the Associated Press. I played alongside another great wide receiver, my boy Quentin Sims, he was the wide receiver on the opposite side of me who really helped inspire and challenge me to continue growing as a player. We were like Goku and Vegeta but our competitive friendship brought out the best in each other, if I and him had played just 1 or 2 more seasons together we would have broke all the college receiving records and would've been all over ESPN and Sports center, no doubt at all. He's actually doing great now and has an amazing story and journey, I plan to convince him to write a book as well. The power of TEAMWORK is just in this, he's actually an editor of this book, and we're working together to help other athletes as well.

All praise to the Most High GOD for blessing my time in college at the University of Tennessee Martin. All the hard work and ups and downs had been worth it and now as a lil kid from Newtown of Sarasota, Florida, the wildest craziest things started to happen. The thing I had been seeking most was seeking me, NFL coaches and teams were pulling me out of class and calling my coaches, and trying to get ahold of me. How crazy is that? The NFL is now looking and interested in little Ole Jeremy Butler. I wasn't drafted but instead, I went undrafted and had multiple teams willing to pay me for my skills. Think about that, to go from not being recruited at all out of high school. To having NFL teams call and offer me bonuses just to agree to come to play for them. I ended up signing on with a bonus to play with the Baltimore Ravens but let me be a kid for a quick second. All my life since I could remember, making it to the NFL is what I wanted to do, and playing against or with some of my favorite players growing up. If you ever played the video game MADDEN, then at some point Ray Lewis was your favorite player just like me. I know you remember that HITSTCICK... I even used to practice his little dance at home and around my family. So here I am walking into the building where one of my favorite players ever Ray Lewis, stamped his legacy. I'm on the team now, granted he was retired by this point but I know he still hangs around the team. I use to be so calm cool and collected in the building keeping my cool but soon as I got home from practice I would call my boys and family super hype about actually being in RAY LEWIS's locker room, I'm actually on the team my favorite player played on. How did this happen? "that's GOD". On the inside, the kid feeling is always there to achieve your dreams, but then the competitor and the fire in you want to compete and show the work you put in and that you're here to play ball. So the NFL is a mix of dream come true for your inner kid but also a battleground where the best of the best are competing with skills they've earned and developed their whole life. That's the part that makes me smile and has my hands sweating getting excited even as I'm writing this, a chance to learn and grow and develop alongside and against the best the world has to offer in my craft. It didn't take me long to adjust to everything and begin to make plays against some of the people I looked up to and admired most. The number one question people ask is "What did it feel like playing in the NFL?" my answer depends on if I'm talking to an athlete or not. If I'm talking to a non-athlete I say "It was everything I wanted as a kid" Fun, and a dream come true, my inner kid answers. My answer for any athletes is different because they understand the work and process that goes into it all, so to other athletes that ask what making it to the NFL is like? I respond "Everything I worked for and a chance to do what I know how to do best, against the best." It's not arrogance because my path has definitely humbled me more than a few times, what I'm expressing is actually faith and confidence. I have faith In God bringing me through so much to be here, it was meant to be, and I have confidence in myself because I know everything I've been through up to this point, I've worked my butt off and earned this.

The NFL showed me and allowed me to grow in ways beyond the sport, it allowed me to travel year-round, and feel the feeling of financial freedom and the ability to help my family and change circumstances around me for the better. I had more time to think and learn different things about myself and life. I felt the truth of what the best version of myself felt like and could be, due to the effort and work it takes to achieve a goal so high. I loved my time in the NFL and I played some great ball, and being able to tell my sons "Daddy did his thing and laced 'em up against the best players in the world" is priceless. I will have the best granddaddy stories in my family, hands down hahaha. The one most important thing the NFL did give me was the PROCESS of the most elite individuals in the world. I learned the process of developing GREATNESS in any area or field of life. Before I share the process I have to share with you the full NFL story.

CHAPTER 13
WARNING: POTENTIAL SIDE EFFECTS

I'm snitching on myself first and loudest, but like MOST of us when we open anything new we never take time to read the instructions or potential side effects. We rush and only focus on the good or the reward we want. If you're like me when I have a headache or toothache I want the pain to stop so bad that 10/10 times I'm not even considering a negative side effect because I'm only focused on getting the pain to stop. Now relate this to a young kid coming from poverty with a broken home and hidden trauma, those circumstances were my non-stop pain, and making it to the NFL was the ultimate painkiller that is supposed to stop it all. That's the mindset coming from the hood and inner-city kids, making it pro is our golden Willy Wonka ticket out of the circumstances. What I learned next is what nobody wants to talk about or seems to wanna share. As an undrafted free agent, I never had the job security of higher draft picks, it's hard to get comfortable when there's the reality that one mistake or injury at the wrong time can end your career or get you shipped out to a new state and city in two days. So I couldn't move my girlfriend and son Jayse up, so essentially I became a part-time dad but full-time NFL player which to some may be fine but for me, going through all I had been through in my childhood and not having a father affected me in ways I didn't have words for. I felt successful as an athlete but felt like a failure as a father, there would be times in the offseason when I'd finally get to go see my son and he didn't even recognize me, he literally wouldn't come to me, or would be scared of me. I had become a stranger to my own son. That alone was enough to make me question myself but now I'm coming into my contract year, which means either I earn another contract with my current team or another team but if not that it could easily be the end of my career. On top of all that, I only knew how to do one thing great, I only had one skill….PLAYING FOOTBALL. I had no idea how to grow all this money I had or how to invest it. So if this is my last year in the NFL then I could easily turn into one of those athletes who go broke and lose EVERYTHING.

CHAPTER 14
WARNING: READ THE LABEL FOR POSSIBLE SIDE EFFECTS

I showed you the difference in performance standards and accountability difference from just JUCO to D1, imagine the difference from college to the Big leagues, the NFL. At this point my anxiety went crazy to the point I had to see a team psychiatrist; my mind was going haywire. Imagine buying the new dream car you wanted all your life and saving up for so long to get it. Then after a few months of owning it, the check engine light, the oil light, and the brake lights all come on at the same time. I had no idea what was happening at the moment but looking back at it, I figured out exactly what was happening. My talent and hard work had introduced me to a level of SUCCESS that my CHARACTER wasn't quite developed to handle. Even though the principles I shared in the first section of the book helped me overcome the struggles within my journey, everything that was happening now was just a professional level of challenge in those same areas of life. There was an NFL level of development with the principles needed from me to maintain this level and standard of life.

Once I had temporarily overcome every previous part of my story, the temporary pain of that chapter made me feel as though I would never deal with it again. Boy, was I wrong!! If you keep taking the pain medicine instead of healing the cause of the pain, sooner or later the pain will outgrow the medicine and create bigger issues. I had temporarily relieved the pain and trauma I was running from by having football success, but the roots of my issues eventually caught back up.

Matthew 19:26 "What profit is it to a man, if he gains the whole world, and lose his soul." One of the most important questions of my life formed in this situation is, "Is my life worth more to me than the NFL?"

Being a successful athlete and finally accomplishing my dreams and "making it" felt amazing but what would be the point of it, if the potential side effects on the important things in me and my son's life were actually sub-par at best? When you factor in the reality that only 2% of athletes ever make it pro and among that 2% majority will never play more than 2 seasons. My journey becomes a lot more relatable and connects to the majority of the players that don't make it or the few guys that do make it beyond a couple of seasons. That's a lot of guys who will or have gone through the same things and I'm sure some will have to answer that same question at some point or another.

What would it profit me to gain and keep fighting for my dreams, while at the same time creating the same environment for my son that I had fought so hard to overcome? I was a great athlete but I wasn't successful in anything that really mattered beyond sports. That's a tough reality that all athletes must face. We all have issues or trauma that we mask with external success, the peace of mind you are looking for success to provide is only found in truly doing the personal self-work that this book addresses. God has a funny way of holding you accountable, he showed me my potential to achieve great worldly success, then gave me something more important to use all that potential and work ethic on in life. I had overcome so many obstacles and worked on my football skills obsessively to reach the NFL, but for the first time in my life something more important than the NFL was settling in my heart, being a great FATHER to my son. If I was capable of achieving all I had on the field and worked so hard for the NFL, was I willing to work just as hard if not harder on being the best man I can be for my son, being the best father I can be? The NFL was exposing the gaps in my life and the work I had ignored, but the NFL and the journey here had given me all the tools to address the issues. So after a couple more years, I was at peace with retiring from the NFL and building off of the life I had created up until this point and the best thing I had earned was a degree from the school of Hard Knocks. A learned the secret formula to SUCCESS in the form of a process.

CHAPTER 15
HIGH 5

The PROCESS is the HIGH-5 principles in part 1 of the book shared already. Elite athletes all over the world develop these areas religiously. From Kobe Bryant, Lebron James, Tom Brady, and Peyton Manning to name a few elite athletes. I even pulled some information from Stephen R. Covey who is an internationally respected figure on the subjects of leadership and success. In his bestselling book "7 Habits of highly effective people" which sold 10 million copies, Stephen lists and defines these traits.

1. Be proactive – Take responsibility and initiative.

2. Begin with the end in mind – work towards a planned future.

3. First things first- decide which tasks are more important when making decisions.

4. Think win-win. Respect and value people, so you can find mutually beneficial solutions.

5. Seek first to understand, then be understood- show empathy by using character, emotions, and credibility.

6. Synergize- work as a team because the sum is greater than any individual member.

7. Sharpen the saw- create sustainable long-term plans. Learn, commit, and do.

Can you see the High-5 principles all within these 7 traits as well? Trust me, they apply to develop greatness in any area or field of life. The key to being and staying successful in ANYTHING is to based on your growth and development as a LEADER in inspiring the best out of others including yourself to a common goal, your RESPONSIBILITY capacity to make the most of resources and situations, your MATURITY in handling and responding to things beyond your control, having COACH-ABILITY that allows you to continuously improve, learn and refine. Once again last but not least your ability to work together and benefit from TEAMWORK. Study as many truly successful people and performers in any career and the results won't change, wherever there's success to be found you can be sure to find these principles right at the foundation of it all. The HIGH-5 principles are super simple but let me be the first to tell you, the trials and struggles I had to experience to learn these principles nearly broke my spirit on a few occasions, but I had to go through it in order to learn how to become a SUCCESSFUL person. If I had control over the pen of my story I would have never written some of the obstacles or adversity within my path, but God has a masterful pen game hahaha and everything that challenged me was exposing where I had gaps to fill as a man, it exposed my weak areas which allowed me to *Fill the Gaps* in my development into manhood and becoming a SUCCESSFUL adult. I touched on it earlier but I wanna say it again for my people's way in the back, "BEING SUCCESSFUL IS NOT WHAT YOU HAVE OR DO, SUCCESS IS WHO YOU ARE AND HOW YOU DO THINGS"

Think of any arena in life like our families, our communities, influence over our kids, business owners, even athletes and performers, think politicians and political leaders, or anything you ever wanted to be in life. All those areas need more;

- **Leaders**-people who inspire and bring the best out of others.

- **Responsibility-** resourceful people who make the best use of all resources and opportunities, and relationships.

- **Maturity**- People who respond well and do not just react to things beyond their control.

- **Coach-Able**- People who are humble enough to learn from and share information, Teach others how to learn from mistakes they've already made.

- **Teamwork**-People who come together through communication and trust to accomplish great things together.

Try to imagine a society and world full of people like this, that's why I'm sharing the secrets I learned from the Elite of the Elite in the sports arena because we need more people like that in these arenas. Everybody deserves to feel true success and let me tell you from the horse's mouth of a professional athlete, no amount of money, success, and or material gain can fill the gaps within yourself, you, and only you can work on and develop yourself. I know from experience.

❧ ❧

CHAPTER 16
WHERE I AM NOW

Since retiring from playing ball, my hands are now full and with a lot of things that bring me joy. First, I want to boldly say without my relationship with the Most High God in christ… none of what I have been through or where I am now would be possible. I'm super blessed and thankful, I have a beautiful wife and family that I'm blessed to serve and lead. I have all the things necessary to say thank you and be grateful daily. The way my life is set up and how I live even all the things I'm involved in if you gave me one wish to have anything or to change anything in my life? I wouldn't change one thing. I'm now mentoring young men and working with student-athletes teaching them personal and life skills through sports, the same HIGH-5 formula in this book. If only 2% of athletes ever make it to Pro and a very small percentage makes enough money in the pros to never have to work again, more attention needs to be paid to developing these young men and women for success beyond sports. Even though I was blessed to be a part of the 2% of athletes that make it pro, I realized the importance of developing skills beyond sports. This is what our program FILL'N THE GAPS does, give each kid the tools for success in the game of life. My son Jayse and me have a podcast as well that you can catch up with us on, Feel free to reach out and check us out and connect us to anyone we may be able to help. Even if there's any advice or help you want to offer, I'm Coachable hahaha.

Here are our social media pages, and me and my son have a podcast where we break down and share real experiences and stories using our HIGH-5 principles daily, great for young children to hear it from another child for perspective. Subscribe to our YOUTUBE channel where we share visual teachings and testimonials.

- www.youtube.com/@Jaybutlersr
- https://fillngaps.com/
- Jay Butler
- Butlerjay1

ACKNOWLEDGEMENTS

This is my favorite part of this book for so many different reasons but mainly because I get to shed some love and light on some really special people in my life. It's pretty simple. The child I was then, the boy I was becoming, and the man I became, I owe all to The Most-High God. When you overcome so many trials and go through so many ups and downs in life, it's easy to get caught up in your own ability and think it's all your doing. Let me be the first to tell you that when I look back over some of the things I've overcome, man I can't even tell you how I made it through. I mean time and time again I passed through situations set up for failure and experiences where there was no chance of success. Even now in my life, the clarity, peace of spirit, wisdom, and grace I move through life with is all of God. Above anything you've learned or could learn in this book even above the HIGH-5 principles, getting your own relationship with God through the belief in Christ is the best thing for your life. All praise to the Most-High.

My uncle Bill, was 1/3 of the big three family unit growing up. I like to tell people all the time if you met my Uncle Bill then you met me and vice versa. It's like he downloaded a carbon copy of his spirit onto me. Both of us got the same humor and funny jokes, we both will give a person the shirt off our backs if it helps them and will do anything for family. I say we but really I mean him, he taught me. I didn't know at the time but the love I was looking for from a father figure was right in front of me. Even though 90% of my childhood scrapes and scars all come from the adventures he would take me on haha-ha, my uncle taught me everything that made me into the man that would even write a book like this. This was the person who put a football in my hand before my pacifier. I know I'm rambling a lil bit but I don't care, this is about my Uncle Bill, let me give him all his flowers. I remember him making me to box kids from other neighborhoods and go on fishing trips with his friends, man he even had me playing tackle football with grown men when I was still in elementary school. I remember we used to watch Monday Night Football every Monday, I'd be up late on school nights, and if Ray Lewis played, every time he made a tackle me and my uncle would do the Ray Lewis dance. I didn't have the childhood I wanted, but he gave me the best childhood I could've had in those times. I went on to play wide receiver and my best talent or skill was my hands, I don't drop the ball at all, THESE HANDS ARE TOO OFFICIAL. Throughout my whole football career I've always been known for catching anything my hand touches, these hands real sticky. Let me share a quick story of how I got like that. My uncle Bill would literally throw footballs at me as hard as he could from about 10-15 yards away. He told me once you stop being scared of being hit or dropping the ball, you'll start to actually catch them. He was right, after dodging them like dodgeballs for a few weeks I finally got over the doubts and started snatching them out of the air, and let me tell you the confidence that came from that was crazy. I snagged my way to the NFL. I owe it to that insane experiment from UNCLE BILL hahaha, you are my HERO, you made me believe I could be the person I am now, I Love you, and THANK YOU.

My Grandma Alice, you always spoke to my soul and spoke life into the things you believed I could accomplish. I have to admit it was balanced with a healthy dose of being popped with your slippers when I would act up hahaha but I appreciate that part just as much as the love. The best thing you ever did for me was teach me to have a relationship with God and how to pray. Those simple instructions changed my life, the little big head boy who your daughter needed help raising would go on to achieve so many great things all from those simple instructions Grandma. Not many people know, I'm probably more of a grandma's baby than a momma's boy. I believe all the wisdom I was blessed with comes from you because when I was only about 5-6 years old, you would talk to me like I was a 35-year-old man about life and people as if I could understand. It's like you prepped me for all the success you believed I would have. The most special trait you have is your ability to connect to people, I've literally witnessed you hold deep and emotional conversations with complete strangers as if they were your best friends. I remember the random pastor we met who was helping us with some directions, a couple of icebreaking jokes and introductions, and boom 15 min later he was crying on your shoulder confessing his life and everything he's been through. In my head, I smiled because he had experienced the magic I had always seen and felt from granny my whole life. The same magic I now know she infused into me as a little kid attached to her hip everywhere she went.

Grandma, you are my guardian Angel and my spiritual rock, I love you eternally. I owe my character, wisdom, and love for people to you.

Ma, like I tell you all the time I'm so proud of you and everything you do and have done. The example you set in front of me inspired so many areas of my life. Our relationship has grown and aligned with every chapter we grow. Seeing you overcome the trials and struggles of poverty, domestic violence, being a single mom and so much more gave me the confidence that "if my mom could overcome all of that, I know I can achieve anything I believe." I carry that attitude into every area of my life even today. Without knowing it you showed me so many traits and qualities that helped me become the best man I could be. The drive to succeed and overcome obstacles I would have never learned or believed in if I hadn't seen you take us from being broke, struggling, and not knowing when our lights or food would run out all the way into a business empire, real estate investor and Educator. Now, look at me with my hands in all the same cookie jars hahaha. So I want you to know just like I always tell you, you did a AMAZING good job raising and bringing me up. The most important thing I picked up from you was my heart to create change, it was always in your heart to help as many people make it through or never have to go through the situations you experienced. That's the one quality where I'm most like you if the book hasn't already made it clear. I witnessed you come from the person in the family who needed the most help and support to now being the one who can provide the most help and support to family and loved ones, and that will forever make you a hero in my eyes. To my heroes hero, Ma I love and appreciate all the inspiration you are to my life, you helped me in so many ways become the person that could write this book and impact the world the way I have been and will. LOVE YOU.

ABOUT THE AUTHOR

If you made it to this point in the book, you should have a
pretty good idea and background of who I am and where I
come from. I hope my story shows you that I'm not much
different than anyone else that is going or will go through a
sports journey. Most people who read this book should see a
lot of themselves in this journey as well. Since this part of the
book is about me, I'll go ahead and share the most important
aspects about me. FAMILY. My wife Danyelle and 3 kids Jayse,
Jeremy jr., and my baby girl Jai'El really make up the foundation of who I am. Fatherhood and a servant to the people I
love. They have all helped and played a role in my growth as
a person to where I am now. Whether by testing my patience;
which seems to be their favorite way hahaha or by opening my
heart to love deeper or by inspiring me to become and do more
to provide and give them the best. This leads me to where I
am currently since retiring from the NFL and settling into the
next chapters of life. As of now I currently mentor young athletes in developing their sports careers and personal lives. This
book you're reading officially makes me an Author and trust
me there are many more books to come. My son Jayse and I
are growing and building a Podcast which you can check out
on YouTube or apple podcasts, where we share deeper sports
concepts and personal development for athletes while sharing

his sports journey being the son of a professional athlete. Also, later this year we are opening our first official family business together, so stay tuned to hear more about that on the podcast and by the next book this section should be even more fun and interesting. While I'm no longer an athlete, sports has taught and developed some principles within me that allow me to be successful in these roles and experiences I'm sharing and that's the theme of this book, I don't know if I would have as much success in Manhood, fatherhood, in my relationships, mentoring others, or as an entrepreneur, author speaker and investor without these principles. Sports can make us so much more than just athletes even though being athletic still helps me get buckets in pickup basketball, there's so much more to sports than just being an athlete and I plan to help as many athletes understand and apply the proof of my life to their lives.